1977

This book m...

FO...

A fine will be charged ...ertime.

GAYLORD 142			PRINTED IN U.S.A.

FRANZ SCHUBERT

COMPLETE CHAMBER MUSIC
FOR PIANOFORTE AND STRINGS

Edited by Ignaz Brüll

———————•———————

FROM THE BREITKOPF & HÄRTEL
COMPLETE WORKS EDITION

DOVER PUBLICATIONS, INC., NEW YORK

Published in Canada by General Publishing Company, Ltd.,
30 Lesmill Road, Don Mills, Toronto, Ontario.
Published in the United Kingdom by Constable and Company, Ltd.,
10 Orange Street, London WC 2.

This Dover edition, first published in 1973, is an unabridged and unaltered re-
publication of *Pianoforte-Quintett, -Quartett und -Trios,* originally published in two
volumes by Breitkopf & Härtel, Leipzig, in 1886 as Series 7 of *Franz Schubert's
Werke. Kritisch durchgesehene Gesammtausgabe.*

International Standard Book Number: 0-486-21527-X
Library of Congress Catalog Card Number: 72-80717

Manufactured in the United States of America
Dover Publications, Inc.
180 Varick Street
New York, N.Y. 10014

Contents

(The dates in parentheses are the years of composition.)

Quintet in A Major, Op. 114 ("Trout")

4

6

7

9

10

11

13

15

20

22

23

24

35

39

40

41

47

Adagio and Rondo Concertant in F Major

54

RONDO.
Allegro vivace.

68

69

76

Trio No. 1 in B-flat Major, Op. 99

80

86

93

95

97

Scherzo.

Allegro.

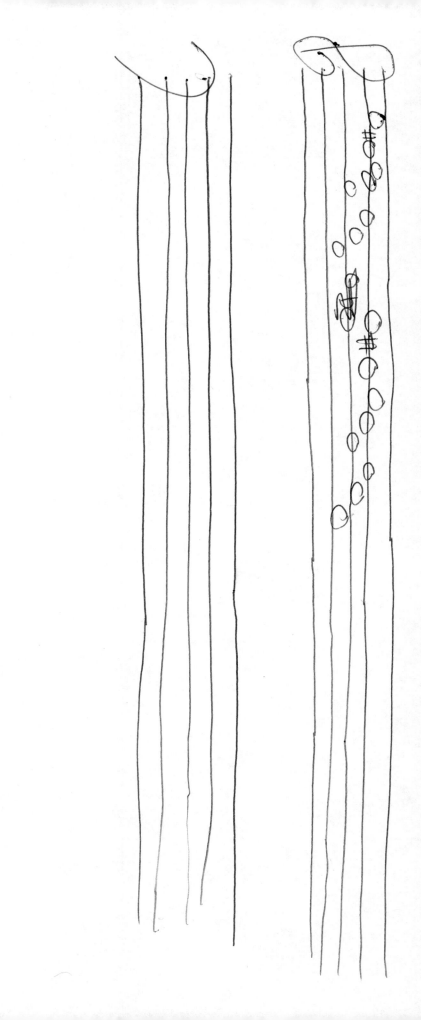

Scherzo da Capo.

Rondo.

Allegro vivace.

Trio No. 2 in E-flat Major, Op. 100

141

147

Scherzo.

Trio.

Scherzo da Capo.

175

179

Notturno in B-flat Major, Op. 148